HAIKUS FOR ADORABLE PRINCESSES

An Illustrated Poetry Book for Our Beloved Little Ones.

CREATED BY:
MAYUMI NAKAGAKI

Copyright© 2024 by Enchanted Tones

All rights reserved. No part of this publication may be reproduced, stored in a retrieval system, or transmitted in any form or by any means, electronic, mechanical, photocopying, recording, or otherwise, without prior written permission from the publisher. Unauthorized replication of this book, including posting to a website, distribution by electronic or physical means, is prohibited and may constitute a violation of applicable laws.

This book, including all brand names and product names mentioned within its pages and on its cover, utilizes trade names, service marks, trademarks, and registered trademarks of their respective owners.

"Haikus for Adorable Princesses - An Illustrated Poetry Book for Our Beloved Little Ones" is primarily a work of fiction and art. The contents, including but not limited to the haikus, illustrations, and themes, are intended for entertainment and educational purposes only. The authors and publishers do not warrant the accuracy, completeness, or usefulness of any information provided and will not be liable for any errors or omissions. This book is not intended to serve as a factual reference but as a source of creative inspiration for children and their guardians. Any interpretation and use of the book's contents are solely at the discretion and risk of the reader.

First Printing Edition, 2024
ISBN: 978-65-983196-2-5

Published by Enchanted Tones
Haikus by Mayumi Nakagaki
Illustrations by Satoshi Watanabe

"ALL WOMEN ARE PRINCESSES, IT IS OUR RIGHT."

— FRANCES HODGSON BURNETT

TABLE OF CONTENTS

CROWN AND COMPANIONS 6

ROYAL GARDENS 8

SILKEN TAPESTRIES 10

MOONLIT WALTZ 12

WHISPERING LIBRARY 14

WINTER HAPPINESS 16

ENCHANTED MIRRORS 18

VELVET CAPES 20

IVORY TOWERS 22

HARVEST FESTIVAL 24

HAIKUS

In a land far, far away, nestled among blossoming cherry trees and towering mountains, there's a special kind of poem called a haiku. Haikus are like tiny treasures, small enough to hold in your hand, but filled with the magic of a big, wide world. They come from Japan, a country rich in history and beauty, where people have been writing haikus for hundreds of years. Imagine a painter using just a few strokes to create a beautiful scene; that's what a haiku does with words.

A haiku is a poem as simple and delightful as a slice of apple pie, but it follows a special recipe. It has only three lines, like three steps on a ladder leading up to a treehouse. The first and last lines have five syllables — like the five fingers on your hand — and the middle line has seven, like the days in a week. Together, these lines capture a moment, a feeling, or a thought, like a snapshot taken with a camera made of words.

Creating a haiku is like going on a treasure hunt. You look around at the world — at the trees, the sky, the animals, and even your feelings — and find something that makes you go "wow!" Then, you take that "wow" and gently wrap it in 17 syllables, choosing your words as carefully as if you were picking flowers for a bouquet. The beauty of a haiku lies in its simplicity and the way it invites us to see the extraordinary in the ordinary. So, grab your word-camera and start your adventure into the wonderful world of haikus!

Mayumi Nakagaki

CROWN AND COMPANIONS

IN CASTLE GARDENS, PLAY,
PRINCESSES LAUGH, ALL DAY,
FRIENDSHIP'S BRIGHT ARRAY.

ROYAL GARDENS

**Morning dew on leaves,
Princesses weave through the trees,
Secret paths they cleave.**

LAUGHTER RINGS IN AIR,
FLORAL CROWNS BEYOND COMPARE,
JOY IN OPEN AIR.

BUTTERFLIES ALIGHT,
ON FINGERS SOFT AND SLIGHT,
NATURE'S DELIGHT, BRIGHT.

SUNSET'S GENTLE CLOSE,
IN GARDENS, PEACE THEY CHOSE,
FRIENDSHIP GROWS, ROSE.

MOONLIT WALTZ

MOONLIT CASTLE HALLS,
ECHOES OF PAST BALLS,
WHERE LAUGHTER RECALLS.

VELVET CAPES

VELVET CAPES, THEY WEAR,
IN THE COOL EVENING AIR,
MYSTERY TO SHARE.

THROUGH THE CASTLE GATE,
SECRET ADVENTURES AWAIT,
EXCITEMENT, THEY SATE.

SHADOWS LONG AND LEAN,
IN THE TWILIGHT, BARELY SEEN,
MAGIC, KEEN, BETWEEN.

THE END

ENCHANTED
TONES

www.ingramcontent.com/pod-product-compliance
Lightning Source LLC
LaVergne TN
LVHW070449120526
838202LV00127B/334